Better English

AGE 7-9

Rhona Whiteford and Jim Fitzsimmons
Illustrated by Sascha Lipscomb

As a parent, your encouragement and involvement can make an important contribution to your child's education. This book is designed to help your child build on the English skills that they have learned at infant school. It will help your child to develop fluency in reading and to learn the simple rules of grammar, punctuation and spelling. There are five tests to help assess your child's progress.

How to help your child

- Keep sessions short and regular. A short period of work every day is usually more effective than a long session once a week.

- Build your child's confidence by offering lots of praise and encouragement. Rather than simply pointing out that an answer is wrong, you could say, 'You were almost right. Let's try again together!'

- As the spoken word is a vital part of learning a language, always discuss what you are doing together and encourage your child to listen and take turns in conversation.

- Don't treat the tests too formally. They are designed to make your child aware of their progress and give them a sense of achievement. You could keep a running total of their results separately and use this to encourage your child.

Hodder
Children's
Books

The only home learning programme supported by the NCPTA

Sentences

A **sentence** is a group of words which makes complete sense on its own.

A. Tick the groups of words which make complete sense on their own.
The first two have been done for you.

1. **the sky is blue today** ✓

2. **this car is** ☐

3. **Sam fell off his bicycle** ✓

4. **my brother has** ☐

5. **I like this book** ✓

6. **blue is my** ☐

Sentences always begin with a capital letter and end with a full stop (.), a question mark (**?**) or an exclamation mark (**!**).

B. Re-write these sentences with capital letters and full stops:

1. **sally was upset when she lost her book**

▶ Sally was upset when she lost her book.

2. **the mechanic repaired the car quickly**

▶ The mechanic repaired the car quickly.

3. **the boy was pleased to win the prize**

▶ The boy was pleased to win the prize.

A sentence which asks something ends with a question mark (**?**). A question can be just one word, e.g. What? Who? When? Why? How? Where? Which?

C. Put a question mark at the end of the sentences below which ask questions:

1. **Where are you going**

2. **This hat is mine** ☐

3. **Who would like cake**

4. **Is this your book** ?

2

This is an **exclamation mark - !** It is used to show strong feelings such as surprise, laughter, happiness, fear, pain or anger. An exclamation can be just one word, e.g. Help! Ouch!

A. Write two more one word exclamations.

1. ▶  !   2. ▶  !

B. Put in an exclamation mark where it is needed in the sentences below:

1. As he fell in the pond, the boy cried out "Help"

2. The children were making lots of noise

3. When the rocket exploded, everyone shouted "Oooh"!

C. Put a full stop, question mark or exclamation mark at the end of each of the following sentences:

1. Where have you left the car

2. The garden looks really beautiful ,

3. The fireman shouted, "Get out now "

4. I really like strawberries and cream .

5. As the ball hit him, he yelled, "Ouch "

6. Which is your umbrella

3

Sentences

Complete these sentences by joining the two halves which go best together:

1. The boy took — his dog for a walk.
2. The bus driver — stopped at the bus stop.
3. Chocolates are — my favourite sweets.
4. The park was — full of beautiful flowers.

Conjunctions

> Words which are used to join short sentences together are called conjunctions, e.g. and, but, as, for, or, yet, then, before, so, that, because, when, after.

A. Use one of the above conjunctions to join these sentences:

1. Sally got up early *because* she had to catch the train.

2. I wanted a shower *but* the water was too cold.

3. He had his breakfast *then* he went for a long walk.

4. I went out to play *after* I had finished my homework.

5. The alarm did not ring *when* he was late for school.

6. He put up his umbrella *and* he went out in the rain.

> Sentences can have different purposes:
>
> A statement — is a sentence which states a fact, e.g. It is very hot.
>
> A question — is a sentence which asks for an answer, e.g. Is it cold outside?
>
> A command — is a sentence which gives an order, e.g. Turn the page.
>
> An exclamation — is a sentence which shows a strong feeling or emotion, e.g. Ouch, that hurt!
>
> A greeting — is a sentence which is used to pass on good wishes, e.g. Good afternoon.

B. Write in each box the kind of sentences you think these are:

1. This is the biggest marrow in the show. ▶ *A statement*

2. Please pick up that litter. ▶ *A command*

3. When does the show start? ▶ *A question*

4. Many happy returns. ▶ *A greeting*

5. Help, get me out of here! ▶ *An exclamation*

6. This shop sells flowers. ▶ *A statement*

7. What is your address? ▶ *A question*

8. Good morning. ▶ *A greeting*

Test 1

Tick the correct sentences:

❶ I can see the castle. ☑   ❷ Please could you ☐

❸ The dog was hungry. ☑

Re-write these sentences with capital letters and full stops:

❹ i am going away on holiday tomorrow

▶ *I'm going away on holiday tomorrow.*

❺ the painting of flowers won first prize

▶ *The painting of flowers won first prize.*

Put in the correct punctuation below:

❻   "Come here now [!] "

❼   My favourite food is pizza [.]

❽   "Did you see that space film last night [?] "

Join the following sentences with a conjunction:

❾   I could see the village *after* the mist cleared.

❿   Mary washed the dishes *and* I dried them.

Write which kind of sentence each of these is in the box provided.

⑪   Keep off the grass. *A command*

⑫   This car is an old wreck. *A statement*

SCORE

6

/12

Nouns

Nouns are words that name people, places and things, e.g. man, house, town, apple.

A. Write out the nouns in each of these sentences.

1. **This apple is ripe and juicy.** ▶ *apple*

2. **The water was frozen solid.** ▶ *water*

3. **The cat was very hungry.** ▶ *cat*

4. **The shop was full of toys.** ▶ *shop*

Proper Nouns - always have a capital letter and are the name of a particular person, place or thing, e.g. London, John, Mercedes.

Common Nouns - do not have capital letters unless they begin a sentence, e.g. book, dog, car.

Sort these words into common and proper nouns. Write each one in the correct column.

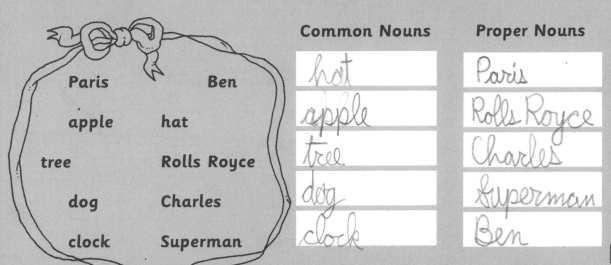

Paris   Ben

apple   hat

tree   Rolls Royce

dog   Charles

clock   Superman

Common Nouns	Proper Nouns
hat	*Paris*
apple	*Rolls Royce*
tree	*Charles*
dog	*Superman*
clock	*Ben*

Collective Nouns

A **collective noun** is the name of a group of people or things which are all of one kind, e.g. a flock of birds, a bunch of flowers.

Complete these lines using one of the words given in this box.

fish
roses   cattle

Add one letter to each word below to make a collective noun.

1. A herd of **cattle**

2. A bed of **roses**

3. A shoal of **fish**

4. A *s*warm of bees

5. A crow*d* of people

6. An arm*y* of soldiers

Pronouns

A word which takes the place of a noun in a sentence is a **pronoun**. Commonly used pronouns are - I, we, me, us, you, he, she, it, they, him, her, them. **Possessive pronouns** are - mine, yours, ours, his, hers, its, theirs.

A. Rewrite these sentences using a <u>pronoun</u> to avoid repeating the noun, e.g. The boy cried out when the boy fell.   The boy cried out when <u>he</u> fell.

1. Sally said that Sally was going to be late.

▶ *Sally said that she was going to be late.*

2. We asked Tom and Jane if Tom and Jane were coming.

▶ *We asked Tom and Jane if they were coming.*

B. Use a possessive pronoun to make these sentences shorter:

1. This coat belongs to him.   This coat is *his*

2. This house belongs to me.   This house is *mine*

Adjectives

An **adjective** is a word which describes a noun. It tells us what the noun is like, e.g. a beautiful face, a cloudy day.

A. Underline the adjective in each phrase:

1. a <u>thrilling</u> race
2. the <u>funny</u> clown
3. a <u>stormy</u> night
4. the <u>haunted</u> castle
5. the <u>wild</u> animal

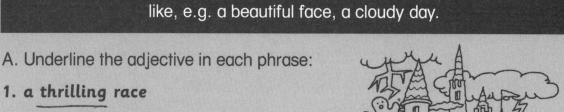

B. Write an adjective to go with these nouns:

1. a *slimy* snake
2. a *famos* book
3. a *blue* sea

Write a noun to go with each adjective below:

4. This huge *ape*
5. The identical *twins*
6. The delicious *Dinner*

C. Write in the space below, the best adjective to describe each noun given, using those provided in the box below.

1. She is a *famos* film actress.

2. The *poor* farmer chased after us.

3. The *black* dog growled and barked.

4. The acrobat wore a *cool* costume.

5. There was a *scary* monster in the film.

| angry | famous | ferocious | slimy | sparkling |

Verbs

Verbs can tell us what a person or thing is doing, e.g. He played the piano.

A. Circle the correct verb from the brackets:

1. The children (smiled/ knocked/ ran) at the door.

2. Laura was (swimming/ painting/ sleeping) in her bed.

3. The caretaker was (smashing/ cleaning/ eating) the windows.

Some verbs are words of being, such as <u>am, is, are,</u> e.g. I am in the garden.

B. Write the verbs <u>am</u>, <u>is</u> or <u>are</u> in the blanks to complete the sentence:

1. Mother _is_ in the sitting room.   2. I _am_ seven years old.

3. _Are_ you a member of the football team?

Word Families

To use verbs in different ways we change the ending e.g. He <u>look</u>s, She <u>look</u>ed, I am <u>look</u>ing. A group of verbs which all share the same root, e.g. <u>look</u>, is called a word family.

I. Complete these word families by adding the endings shown:

Root verb	add 's'	add 'ed'	add 'ing'
laugh	laugh's	laughed	laughing
pull	pull	pulled	pulling
act	acts	acted	acting

Adverbs

Adverbs tell us more about the verb in a sentence. They describe how actions are done, e.g. Peter <u>walked</u> quickly. The adverb, <u>quickly</u>, tells us how Peter walked.　　　　(verb)　(adverb)

A. Draw a line under the verb, and a ring around the adverb in each sentence.

1. I listened carefully.

2. He shouted angrily.

3. The car stopped suddenly.

4. The engine rattled noisily.

Adverbs are made by adding **ly** to an adjective, e.g. quick (adjective) becomes quickly (adverb). If an adjective ends in the letter **y** it becomes an adverb by adding **il** in front of the **y**, e.g. sleepy (adjective) becomes sleepily (adverb).

B. Complete each sentence with an adverb, made from the adjective on the left.

1. clear　　　　We could see   from the cliff top.

2. careful　　　The children crossed the road   .

3. quiet　　　　We crept   into the library.

4. soft　　　　The cat landed   on the grass.

5. brave　　　The fireman fought the fire   .

6. happy　　　The children smiled   for the

photographer.

TEST 2

1 Underline the nouns in these sentences:

    a) The dog chased after the cat. b) The boat sailed away over the sea.

2 Write two common nouns below:

    a) ▶ [   ]   **b)** ▶ [   ]

3 Write two proper nouns below:

    a) ▶ [   ]   **b)** ▶ [   ]

4 Fill in the gaps below with the right collective noun:

    a) A [   ] **of bees**   **b) A** [   ] **of people**

5 Underline the pronouns in these sentences:

    a) The gardener promised he would cut the grass.

    b) This coat is hers.

6 Underline the adjectives in these sentences:

    a) We watched an exciting film. b) The scruffy dog rolled in the grass.

7 Underline the verbs in these sentences:

    a) The policeman stopped the car. b) I am the son of a doctor.

8 Make adverbs from these adjectives:

    a) noisy ▶ [   ]   **b) graceful** ▶ [   ]

9 Add a verb with the right ending to make sense of the sentences below:

    a) I always [   ] **to school.**   **b) I** [   ] **my tea quickly this afternoon.**

10 Write out the word family for the verb <u>talk</u>:

SCORE

/10

12

Commas

This is a **comma - ,**. We use it when there is a list of words in a sentence. We separate each word with a comma. The last word in the list is usually joined to it by the word <u>and</u> instead of a comma, e.g. We need paper, paint, glue <u>and</u> scissors.

A. Put commas in these sentences:

1. At the zoo we saw lions tigers monkeys and elephants.

2. There was a huge pile of hats coats scarves shoes and socks.

3. The colours of the rainbow are red orange yellow green blue

   indigo and violet.

The comma can also be used to mark a short pause inside a sentence. It is used to separate two words, or groups of words, in a sentence, to make the meaning clearer, e.g. After we had been to the park, we went to the café.

B. Put a comma in these sentences:

1. Once the box was opened we could see inside.

2. The window was smashed to pieces so she ran away.

3. With all the heavy rain the garden was flooded.

Apostrophes

A comma written above the line is called an **apostrophe**. We can use an apostrophe to show that some letters have been missed out, e.g. Do not = Don't, We are = We're, What is = What's, You will = You'll, I will = I'll, I am = I'm.

A. Write the shortened form of these words by leaving out the letters underlined and putting in an apostrophe instead. The first one has been done for you.

1. let <u>us</u>   let's   8. could n<u>o</u>t

2. we <u>had</u>   9. has n<u>o</u>t

3. can<u>no</u>t   10. would n<u>o</u>t

4. it <u>is</u>   11. did n<u>o</u>t

5. we <u>will</u>   12. have n<u>o</u>t

6. I <u>have</u>   13. we <u>a</u>re

7. should <u>ha</u>ve   14. she <u>is</u>

An apostrophe can be used to show something belongs to someone.

| If there is only one owner of an object, we add the apostrophe and **s** to show something belongs, e.g. John's coat. | When there is a group of people - <u>the boys</u> - owning a set of things - <u>coats</u> - the apostrophe comes after the **s** or **es**, e.g. The boys' coats. |

B. Put in the apostrophe below:

1. Sally s bag.   4. The cats baskets.

2. Father s chair.   5. The ladies hats.

3. The girl s hat.   6. The ships sails.

14

Inverted commas

There are two ways of writing down what someone says. If we write down the exact words spoken it is called **direct speech**. If we repeat what they said in our own words it is called **indirect speech**.

e.g. Fred said, "I am late."   Fred said that he was late.
(Direct speech)   (Indirect speech)

A. Put a ring around the sentences in direct speech and underline those in indirect speech:

1. Jack said that he really liked his present.

2. May I go out to play? asked Ben.

3. What time is it? asked Alex.

4. Mum asked me if I would go to the shops.

Words that are actually spoken are written inside inverted commas, also known as speech marks or quotation marks. These (") go at the beginning of the speech, and these (") go at the end. The spoken words start with a capital letter, e.g. " These are my gloves," said Pam.

B. Draw a ring around the words which are actually spoken, then re-write the sentence using inverted commas.

1.   I am going out to play, said Helen.

▶   "I am going out to play," said Helen.

2.   This is my favourite game, said Lynne.

▶

3.   I like watching television, said Roger.

▶

■ TEST 3 ■

Put commas in the following sentences:

❶ On the motorway we saw cars lorries buses and wagons.

❷ At the stationery shop I bought pencils paper rubbers and glue.

❸ In the circus parade we saw clowns acrobats jugglers and animals.

❹ We had lunch then we went shopping.

❺ Before going to bed I had a bath.

Put the apostrophes in below:

❻ Sam s dog

❼ Mother s hat

❽ Mary s car

❾ Tom s book

❿ Grandmother s shawl

⓫ the babies prams

⓬ the footballers shirts

⓭ the ladies handbags

⓮ the boys pencils

⓯ the soldiers uniforms

Put in the inverted commas where they are needed:

⓰ May I come to the party too? asked William.

⓱ Sarah said that she had lost her favourite book.

⓲ It is my birthday today, said the old man.

⓳ The shopkeeper said, I am closing early tomorrow.

⓴ The doctor told the patient that he was much better.

SCORE

/20

Singular or plural

A **singular** word talks about one thing or one group, e.g. one cow or one herd of cows. There are many spelling rules for changing a word from singular to plural. A **plural** talks about many things or groups of things.

A simple rule. Most words just add 's', e.g. cat changes to cats.

1. Write the plural of these words:

doctor [   ]   tree [   ]   hose [   ]   flute [   ]

Words ending in s, x, ch, tch, sh, add 'es', e.g. bus changes to buses.

2. Make these words plural:

fox [   ]   brush [   ]   match [   ]   torch [   ]

church [   ]   kiss [   ]   watch [   ]   peach [   ]

Words ending in y. If there is a vowel before the 'y' add 's'. If there is a consonant before the 'y' change 'y' to 'i' and add 'es', e.g. puppy becomes puppies.

3. Write the plural of these words:

army [   ]   tray [   ]   toy [   ]

cherry [   ]   quay [   ]   memory [   ]

Words ending in f or fe. Most f and fe plurals end in 'ves', e.g. leaf changes to leaves. Remember ff words just add 's'.

4. Change these words to the plural:

wolf [   ]   cliff [   ]   wife [   ]

calf [   ]   ruff [   ]   knife [   ]

Silent letters

'h' is often silent after a 'w', e.g. <u>wh</u>ale

Put the silent 'h' in the spaces below to complete the words:

w__en   w__ether   w__at   w__ere   w__im

w__y   w__ile   w__ite   w__ich   w__elk

'h' is also silent after a 'g', e.g. <u>gh</u>ost.
Sometimes both letters are silent, e.g. ni<u>gh</u>t.

Add gh to the gaps below and draw a line to match with the right clue.

1. hi___   A. The opposite of dark

2. si___   B. A girl child is a _____

3. bri___t   C. A light breath.

4. dau___ter   D. Opposite of dull.

5. li___t   E. Opposite of low.

Shade in the silent letter of the words below. Write another word in each box, using the same silent letters e.g. calf and half.

calf	comb	wren	know	gnat	rhythm
l	f	m	b	w	r	k	n	g	n	r	h

Double letters

We sometimes use double letters to spell a single sound e.g. se**ll**, cli**ff**. They usually appear after a short vowel sound e.g. pa**tt**er, sme**ll**, mi**ll**, cro**ss**, su**pp**er, but not after a long vowel sound e.g. g**a**te, f**ee**t, m**i**le, b**o**ne, l**u**te.

1. Write two more words using these double letters:

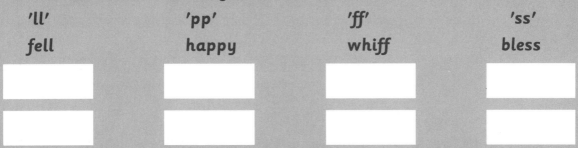

'll'	'pp'	'ff'	'ss'
fell	happy	whiff	bless

2. Pick the correct spelling for these words:

bu ___ (z / zz)   fu ___ y (n / nn)   a ___ ear (p / pp)

bee ___ (f / ff)   bu ___ le (b / bb)   usua ___ y (l / ll)

Hard or soft sounds

'c' can be soft and sound like 's', as in cinema, or hard as in cake.
'g' can be soft and sound like 'j', as in gym, or hard as in get.

Write 'h' for hard or 's' for soft next to these words:

Write 3 words for each in the columns below:

general		gun		soft 'c'	soft 'g'
cygnet		gone			
ceiling		cattle			
cable		gentle			
gesture		cement			

TEST 4

Write the plurals of these words:

❶ wolf

❷ cake

❸ chicken

❹ berry

❺ sash

❻ country

Write the singular of these words:

❼ boxes

❽ watches

❾ memories

❿ knives

⓫ pigs

⓬ churches

Use the clue to find a word using the silent letters given:

⓭ A medieval soldier   kn

⓮ A broken ship   wr

⓯ Fixes burst pipes   mb

Double Letters. Unravel the letters to find a word:

⓰ lifcf

⓱ aphpy

⓲ sems

SCORE

/18

Joined-up handwriting

Joined-up handwriting helps you learn to spell! The flow and joined pattern helps fix the **letter string** in your mind.

Practise these strings in your school style.

ight ide dge age tion ought aught

Letter strings

Letter strings are letters that appear grouped together in different words and always sound the same, e.g. -ight, -dge, -ought.

tion as in station

Add the letter string, then write the whole word.

1. ac_____ ▶

2. por_____ *tion* ▶

3. ra_____ ▶

age and *dge* , as in marriage and ledge, are found at the end of words.

Sort these words out:

age	*dge*

hedge   passage

voyage

judge   bridge

manage

wedge   damage

sausage

21

More letter strings

able as in sta<u>ble</u>. Fill in the missing words below:

1. A plant we eat is a   v _ _ _ _ _ _ _

2. A place to keep a horse is a   s _ _ _ _ _

3. We sit at a   t _ _ _ _   to eat.

4. We are   c _ _ _ _ _ _ _ _ _   when we feel restful and cosy.

ight as in night is a common word ending.

Make word crosses for these words ending in -ight.

knight
sight
light
might
tonight
right

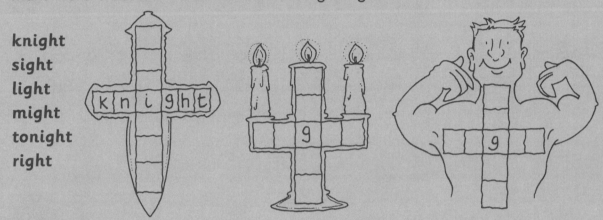

ought and *aught* usually sound the same and we simply have to remember when each is used.

Sort these words into the right columns according to their endings:

aught   *ought*

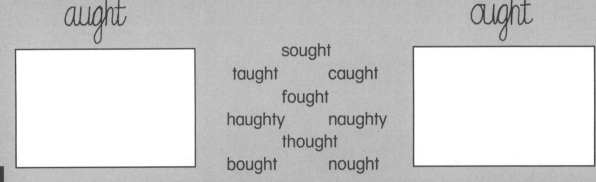

sought
taught   caught
fought
haughty   naughty
thought
bought   nought

Beginnings

Sometimes a group of letters is added to the beginning of a word to change its meaning. This is called a **prefix**. Adding a prefix is easy, there is no need to drop any letters, e.g. mis + spell = misspell. All and well are different. They drop an l when they are added to the beginning of a word, e.g. all + together = altogether and well + come = welcome.

Opposites

Some prefixes change a word to its opposite meaning.
Match these prefixes to the words below to change their meaning:

PREFIXES			WORDS		
mis	dis	un	take	appoint	do
non	in	im	sense	expensive	proper

Now list the new words you have made:

1. ▶
2. ▶
3. ▶
4. ▶
5. ▶
6. ▶

Add some of the prefixes suggested above to the words in the following passage to change the meaning:

I had been the most ...... obedient child in class all term. My teacher thought it ...... likely that the headteacher would reward me for my .... behaviour. My mother agreed that that would be ...... possible.

NUMBER PREFIXES		
uni	-	one
bi	-	two
tri	-	three
poly	-	many
multi	-	many

Draw a line to join each prefix to one word on the right.

uni   -angle
bi   -gon
tri   -coloured
poly   -cycle
multi   - corn

23

Endings

Some suffixes change the way a verb can be used, e.g. talk + <u>ed</u> = talk<u>ed</u>. This changes I talk (present tense) to I talk<u>ed</u> (past tense). (see Word Families on page 10.)

Choose the right verb ending to make sense of the sentences below:

a) Mum (smile/ smiles/ smiling) when she sees me.
b) We (visit/ visits/ visited) my friend today.
c) My family (enjoys/ enjoyed/ enjoying) going to the cinema.

Some suffixes change a word into an adjective.

WORD	SUFFIX	NEW WORD (ADJECTIVE)	SENTENCE
fright ⟶	ful ⟶	frightful	He looks frightful
care ⟶	less		
self ⟶	ish		
delight ⟶	ful		

Some suffixes change a word into a type of noun.

Suffix	Add the correct suffix to complete the sentences.
-er	1. There is great friend............ within the team.
-hood	2. Our swimming teach............ is great.
-ship	3. My dad started a neighbour............ watch scheme.

Unusual words

Can you write the meanings for each of these homophones below?

1. boy - | a male child |

   buoy - | a floating marker |

3. hair - | |

   hare - | |

2. key - | |

   quay - | |

4. pain - | |

   pane - | |

Fill the gaps in these sentences with the correct homophone:

5. I can _____ very neatly. (write / right)

6. I'd love a _____ of cake. (piece / peace)

7. I quickly let go of the _____ . (rein / reign)

Write two sentences for each of these words to show the different meanings:

watch 1. ▶ _____

        2. ▶ _____

light 1. ▶ _____

        2. ▶ _____

hatch 1. ▶ _____

        2. ▶ _____

■ TEST 5 ■

LETTER STRINGS. The three answers below share the same letter string. Guess the word and write it out in joined-up handwriting:

❶ Opposite of left [   ]   **❷** Opposite of loose [   ]

❸ Opposite of depth [   ]

PREFIXES. Change these words to their opposite meaning by adding a prefix:

❹ sense ▶[   ]   **❺** do ▶[   ]

❻ like ▶[   ]

SUFFIXES. Add a suffix to these words to make a noun which means a worker doing each of these jobs:

❼ paint ▶[   ]   **❽** farm ▶[   ]

❾ engine ▶[   ]

HOMOPHONES. These words sound the same but only one is spelt right for the sentence. Underline the right words below:

❿ The owl hooted outside the window all knight / night.

⓫ The doctor said she needed to way / weigh me.

⓬ I am learning to sew / so.

HOMONYMS. There are two meanings for each of these words. Write a sentence for each of them:

⓭ train [   ] [   ]

⓮ mould [   ] [   ]

⓯ flat [   ] [   ]

SCORE

/15

26

Finding information

We store information in computers, books, directories, dictionaries, encyclopaedias and libraries and we store this information alphabetically. This means we need to know the alphabet to find the information in these places.

A. Quickly fill in the missing letters:

A B _ _ E F _ H _ _ K L M _ _ _ P Q _ S _ U _ W X _ Z

a _ _ d _ f g _ i j _ l m n _ _ _ r s _ u v _ x y _

B. Use a dictionary to find:

3 words starting with 'M'   3 five letter words

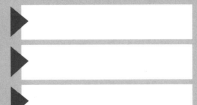   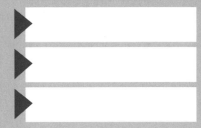

The longest word you can find: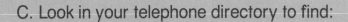

C. Look in your telephone directory to find:

1. **The phone number of a toy shop.**

2. **The phone number of a relative or friend.**

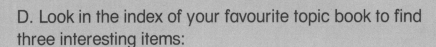

D. Look in the index of your favourite topic book to find three interesting items:

Book:	
	Item 1 _____ page ___
	Item 2 _____ page ___
	Item 3 _____ page ___

Reading with understanding

Read the passage below then answer the questions about it.

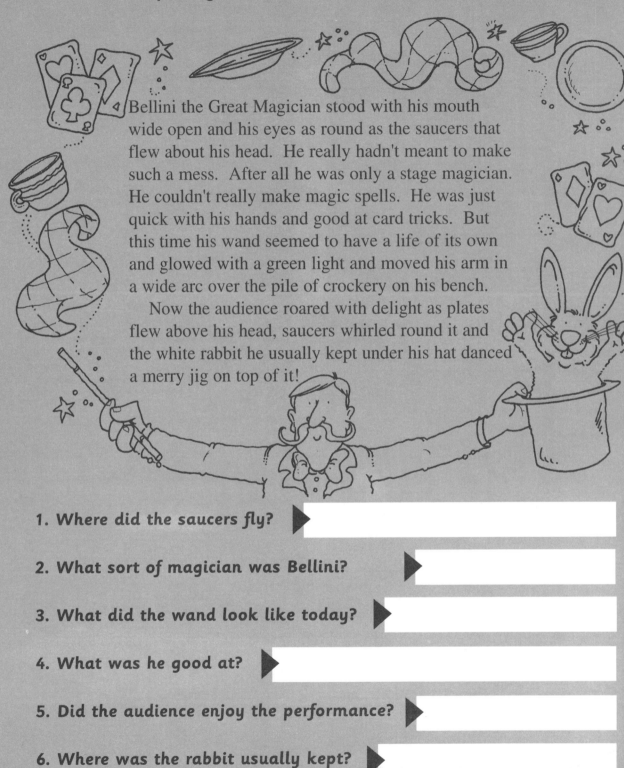

Bellini the Great Magician stood with his mouth wide open and his eyes as round as the saucers that flew about his head. He really hadn't meant to make such a mess. After all he was only a stage magician. He couldn't really make magic spells. He was just quick with his hands and good at card tricks. But this time his wand seemed to have a life of its own and glowed with a green light and moved his arm in a wide arc over the pile of crockery on his bench.

Now the audience roared with delight as plates flew above his head, saucers whirled round it and the white rabbit he usually kept under his hat danced a merry jig on top of it!

1. Where did the saucers fly?

2. What sort of magician was Bellini?

3. What did the wand look like today?

4. What was he good at?

5. Did the audience enjoy the performance?

6. Where was the rabbit usually kept?

Reading with care

Some words have been left out of the passage. In some cases only one word will do to make it read correctly, but in other cases you can choose from several words to give the writing a new meaning.

   Read through the passage quickly to get an idea of the meaning, then read more carefully, trying out some of the words listed in the box below. When you are satisfied with your choice, write it in the spaces below and read the passage through again.

The visitors

Slowly and steadily the ------------- craft settled just above ------------ level

and hovered there silently. A doorway materialized ------------- the side and

from it --------------- a shimmering ramp. From their hiding place behind the

bushes, the children stared in ------------------ as two circles of light appeared at

the doorway and moved down the ramp ------------------. As they moved they

formed into figures, small but of ------------- shape and with the most ----------

faces. It was obvious that ------------- planet was strange and new to them.

They --------------------- around with wondering eyes and, holding hands,

---------------- stepped on to the grass. The children gasped as the creatures

looked in ---------------- direction and, smiling, moved towards ----------------

bushes with arms outstretched in greeting.

The words in the box are arranged in the same order as the spaces in the passage. Where you have a choice, suggested words are grouped together but you may use your own ideas if you want to.

space	alien		ground	roof	in
stretched	shot	glided	terror	astonishment	horror
together	slowly	silently	human	strange	alien
beautiful	terrible	unusual	this		
looked	glared	stared	they	their	the

29

Answers

Page 2
A. 1, 3 and 5 form sentences.

B. 1. Sally was upset when she lost her book.
2. The mechanic repaired the car quickly.
3. The boy was pleased to win the prize.

C. 1. Where are you going?
3. Who would like cake?
4. Is this your book?

Page 3
B. 1. As he fell in the pond the boy cried out "Help!"
2. The children were making lots of noise.
3. When the rocket exploded, everyone shouted "Oooh!"

C. 1. Where have you left the car?
2. The garden looks really beautiful.
3. The fireman shouted, "Get out now!"
4. I really like strawberries and cream.
5. As the ball hit him, he yelled, "Ouch!"
6. Which is your umbrella?

Page 4
1. The boy took his dog for a walk.
2. The bus driver stopped at the bus stop.
3. Chocolates are my favourite sweets.
4. The park was full of beautiful flowers.

A. 1. because/as 2. but
3. before/then
4. when/after/before
5. so
6. when/before/then

(There are different alternatives for some of the above answers - at the marker's discretion)

Page 5
B. 1. Statement
2. Command
3. Question
4. Greeting
5. Exclamation
6. Statement
7. Question
8. Greeting

Page 6
TEST 1

1 & 3 are correct sentences.
4. I am going away on holiday tomorrow.
5. The painting of flowers won first prize.
6. "Come here now!"
7. My favourite food is pizza.
8. " Did you see that space film last night?"
9. I could see the village when/after the mist cleared.
10. Mary washed the dishes so/as/while/then/and/but I dried them.
11. Command
12. Statement

Page 7
A. 1. apple 2. water
3. cat   4. shop, toys
Common Nouns - apple, tree, dog, clock, hat
Proper Nouns - Paris, Ben, Rolls Royce, Charles, Superman

Page 8
1. cattle 2. roses 3. fish
4. swarm 5. crowd
6. army

A. 1. Sally said that she was going to be late.
2. We asked Tom and Jane if they were coming.

B. 1. This coat is his.
2. This house is mine.

Page 9
A. 1. thrilling 2. funny
3. stormy
4. haunted 5. wild

C. 1. famous 2. angry
3. ferocious
4. sparkling 5. slimy

Page 10
A. 1. knocked 2. sleeping
3. cleaning

B. 1. is 2. am 3. are
1. laughs, laughed, laughing
pulls, pulled, pulling
acts, acted, acting

Page 11

A. 1. listened (verb)
       carefully (adverb)
    2. shouted (verb) angrily
       (adverb)
    3. stopped (verb)
       suddenly (adverb)
    4. rattled (verb) noisily
       (adverb)

B. 1. clearly   2. carefully
    3. quietly   4. softly
    5. bravely   6. happily

Page 12

TEST 2

1a) dog, cat   1b) boat, sea
4a) swarm   4b) crowd
5a) he   5b) hers
6a) exciting   6b) scruffy
7a) stopped   7b) am
8a) noisily   8b) gracefully
10. talk, talks, talked, talking

Page 13

A. 1. At the zoo we saw
       lions, tigers, monkeys
       and elephants.
    2. There was a huge pile
       of hats, coats,
       scarves, shoes and
       socks.
    3. The colours of the
       rainbow are red,
       orange, yellow, green,
       blue, indigo and violet.

B. 1. Once the box was
       opened, we could see
       inside.
    2. The window was
       smashed to pieces,
       so she ran away.

    3. With all the heavy
       rain, the garden was
       flooded.

Page 14

A. 1. let's   2. we'd
    3. can't   4. it's
    5. we'll   6. I've
    7. should've
    8. couldn't
    9. hasn't   10. wouldn't
   11. didn't   12. haven't
   13. we're   14. she's

B. 1. Sally's   2. Father's
    3. girl's   4. cats'
    5. ladies'   6. ships'

Page 15

A. 1 & 4 - indirect
    2 & 3 - direct
    "May I go out to play?"
    asked Ben.
    "What time is it?"
    asked Alex.

B. 2. "This is my favourite
       game," said Lynne.
    3. "I like watching
       television," said Roger.

Page 16

TEST 3

1. On the motorway we saw
    cars, lorries, buses and
    wagons.
2. At the stationery shop I
    bought pencils, paper,
    rubbers and glue.
3. In the circus parade we
    saw clowns, acrobats,
    jugglers and animals.
4. We had lunch, then we
    went shopping.
5. Before going to bed, I
    had a bath.

    6. Sam's dog
    7. Mother's hat
    8. Mary's car
    9. Tom's book
   10. Grandmother's shawl
   11. the babies' prams
   12. the footballers' shirts
   13. the ladies' handbags
   14. the boys' pencils
   15. the soldiers' uniforms
   16. "May I come to the party
       too?" asked William.
   17. Sarah said that she had
       lost her favourite book.
   18. "It is my birthday today,"
       said the old man.
   19. The shopkeeper said,
       "I am closing early
       tomorrow."
   20. The doctor told the
       patient that he was much
       better.

Page 17

1. doctors, trees, hoses,
    flutes
2. foxes, brushes, matches,
    torches, churches,
    kisses, watches, peaches
3. armies, trays, toys,
    cherries, quays,
    memories
4. wolves, cliffs, wives,
    calves, ruffs, knives

Page 18

1. high E   2. sigh C
3. bright D   4. daughter B
5. light A
silent letters: l, b, w, k, g, h

Page 19

2. buzz, funny, appear,
    beef, bubble, usually.

Hard sounds - cable, gun, gone, cattle

Soft sounds - general, cygnet, ceiling, gesture, gentle, cement

Page 20
TEST 4
1. wolves
2. cakes
3. chickens
4. berries
5. sashes
6. countries
7. box
8. watch
9. memory
10. knife
11. pig
12. church
13. knight
14. wreck
15. plumber
16. cliff
17. happy
18. mess

Page 22
1. vegetable
2. stable
3. table
4. comfortable

Page 23
mistake, disappoint, undo, nonsense, inexpensive, improper

dis - obedient un - likely
mis - behaviour
im - possible
unicorn, bicycle, triangle, polygon, multicoloured

Page 24
a) smiles   b) visited
c) enjoys

friendship, teacher, neighbourhood

Page 25
2. key – an instrument for locking or unlocking.
   quay – a landing place for boats.
3. hair – a fibre growing from the skin.
   hare - a swift mammal, larger than a rabbit.
4. pane – a piece of window glass.
   pain – suffering.
5. write   6. piece
7. rein

Page 26
TEST 5
1. right
2. tight
3. height
4. nonsense
5. undo
6. dislike
7. painter
8. farmer
9. engineer
10. night
11. weigh
12. sew
13. steam train or train for athletics
14. mould grew on the ceiling or mould a pot from clay.
15. buy a flat or squash flat.

Page 28
1. about his head
2. stage magician
3. It glowed with a green light.
4. card tricks
5. yes
6. under his hat

Copyright © 1995 Rhona Whiteford and Jim Fitzsimmons

The right of Rhona Whiteford and Jim Fitzsimmons to be identified as the authors of this work has been asserted by them in accordance with the Copyright, Design and Patent Act 1988.

First published in Great Britain 1995

Published by Hodder Children's Books, a division of Hodder Headline plc, 338 Euston Road, London NW1 3BH.
Printed in Great Britain.

A CIP record is registered by and held at the British Library.

Spelling

AGE 7-9

Dr Bill Gillham
Illustrated by Sascha Lipscomb

Spelling is a neglected skill; yet nothing makes a worse impression than a badly spelt letter or exam answer. This book is designed to help your child learn the techniques and master the useful rules of this vital skill. In English no 'rule' about spelling is 100% true, but if it works 90–95% of the time, it is worth learning.

How to help your child

● Keep sessions short and regular: learning is better when it is spaced out.

● Practise the Look – Copy – Cover – Write – Check technique (see page 4) which develops visual memory – important when words often don't spell as they sound.

● Encourage your child to keep a spelling notebook of words they get wrong at school, and to learn them (five a day) using the same technique.

● Sometimes you will need to involve yourself in the exercises so that your child can hear the words pronounced. Listening is an important part of learning to spell.

● **Reading helps spelling:** so make sure that your child has plenty of books to read.

● **Praise success**, and don't treat the tests too formally. They are designed to make your child aware of their progress and give them a sense of achievement.

Hodder Children's Books

The only home learning programme supported by the NCPTA

Spell as you say

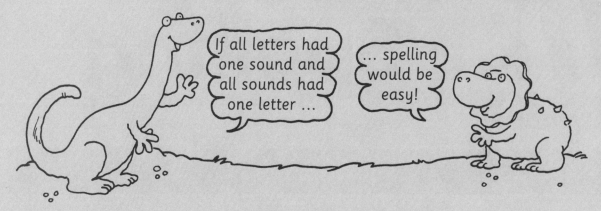

Write the words for these pictures in the boxes underneath.
They are all three-letter words.

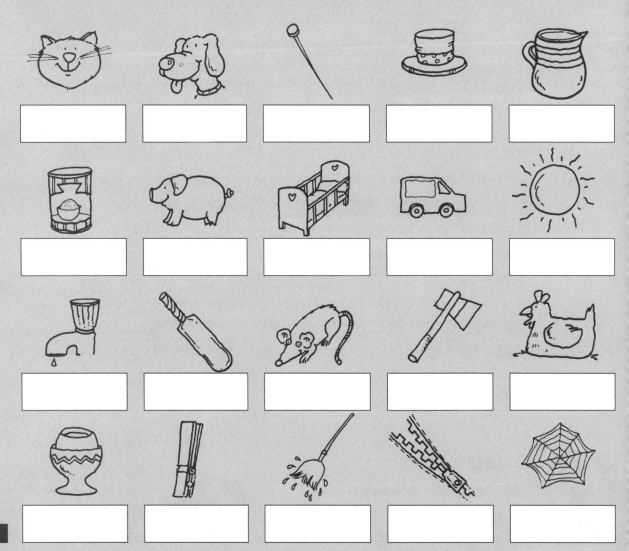

If you say the syllables slowly as you write a word, you will often spell it right.
Write the words underneath these pictures.

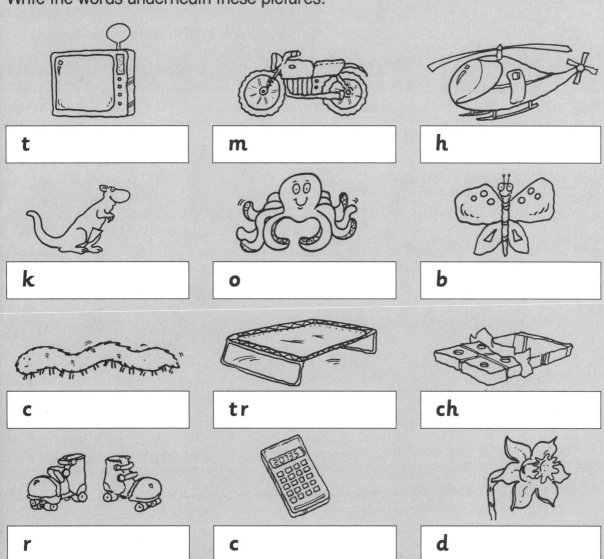

t ___

m ___

h ___

k ___

o ___

b ___

c ___

tr ___

ch ___

r ___

c ___

d ___

Check on page 32 to see whether you are exactly right or nearly right.

Spell as you see

Some words don't **sound** as they **look**.

Like this:

It sounds like **yot** but it's spelt **yacht**!

You have to **learn** how they **look**.

… and here's how to do it!

- **Look** at the word

yacht

- **Copy** it on a separate piece of paper.

yach

- **Cover** it over so you can't see it.

- **Write** the word again.

yoct

yacht

- Uncover and **check**.

yocht

yacht

Keep doing it until you get it right!

4

Now practise with these words. Do them one at a time.

● Look	definite	foreign	visitor	surprise	really
● Copy					
● Cover					
● Write					
● Check ✔ or ✗	◯	◯	◯	◯	◯

Repeat any you get wrong.

Now try these words.

● Look	paid	height	medicine	science	success
● Copy					
● Cover					
● Write					
● Check ✔ or ✗	◯	◯	◯	◯	◯

Keep repeating any you get wrong, until you have got them right.

More spell as you see

Learn these ten words in balloons.
When you've learnt a word, burst the balloon!

Start again if
you've got it
wrong!

said

around

many

caught

exercise

father

interest

knee

early

address

Now use the ten words you've learnt.
Look at them all again **once**, cover them over, and put them in the gaps here:

1. My [_____] hurt his [_____] .

2. I got up [_____] and [_____] the first bus.

3. [_____] people don't take any [_____] .

4. 'Give me your [_____],' he [_____], 'and I'll
   write to you.'

5. There is a lot of [_____] in football [_____] here.

6

Here are twelve words in cakes to learn.
When you've learnt the word, eat the cake!

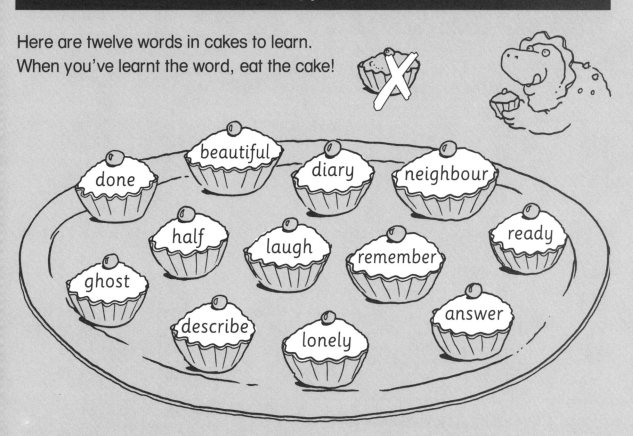

Now use the twelve words you've learnt.
Look at them all again **once**, cover them over, and then correct these spellings:

dun	neihgbor	redy	gost

diairy	beatifull	hafl	remeber

discribe	largh	arnser	lonly

7

Sound-alikes

Some words **sound** the same but **mean** something different.

To the adult:
Talk your child through this page.

Here are some examples:

buy   Will you **buy** me a coke?

by   This workbook is **by** Bill Gillham.

four   Our cat had **four** kittens.

for   This kitten is **for** you.

hole   This bucket has a **hole** in it.

whole   I ate a **whole** bar of chocolate.

their   They were wearing **their** best clothes.

there   Put the shopping over **there**.

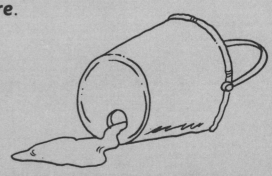

no   I had **no** money at all.

know   Do you **know** my name?

With **sound-alikes** you have to know what they **mean** to spell them the right way.

Looking at the list of sound-alikes on the left page, see if you can do these.

Cross out the word that is wrong.

1. I have ┌ *for/four* ┐ brothers and sisters.

2. I am going to ┌ *by/buy* ┐ some new trainers.

3. ┌ **There/their** ┐ father took them to school.

4. The letter had ┌ **no/know** ┐ stamp on it.

5. The ┌ **hole/whole** ┐ class had a special treat.

6. We went to London ┌ **by/buy** ┐ train.

7. This present is ┌ **for/four** ┐ you.

8. I've got a ┌ **whole/hole** ┐ in my jeans.

9. Mum's car is over ┌ **their/there** ┐ .

10. I ┌ **know/no** ┐ how to do this puzzle.

Pick a word from the sound-alikes above to fill each gap.

1. My little brother can only count up to ┌   ┐ .

2. Our house is ┌   ┐ the station.

3. I ┌   ┐ a lot about horses.

4. I put it ┌   ┐ on the table.

5. I gave our cat a ┌   ┐ tin of cat food.

Plural endings

One of something is
SINGULAR

More than one is
PLURAL

one **spider**

lots of **spiders**

To make a singular word plural, you mostly just add **s.**
But if the word ends in:
x, **s**, **sh**, **ch**, **o** – add **es.**

Like this:

| box**es** | cross**es** | dish**es** | church**es** | potato**es** |

Write the plurals of these:

1.	tomato___	6.	tap___	11.	address___
2.	wish___	7.	table___	12.	torch___
3.	echo___	8.	princess___	13.	shoe___
4.	window___	9.	fox___	14.	match___
5.	present___	10.	brush___	15.	bus___

But the plural of
piano is pian**os**!

To the adult: Using a separate piece of paper, test the spellings learnt on pages 6 and 7. Score 1 for each correct word: and practise any spelt incorrectly.

SCORE

/ 22

Spelling by rules

i before *e* except after *c*

bel<u>ie</u>ve but **rec<u>ei</u>ve**

<u>except</u> for:

their	weird	(n)either	
eight	weight	height	science
seize	reign	foreign	

Fill **ie** or **ei** into the gaps in these words:

1. dec _ _ ve

2. t _ _ d

3. f _ _ ld

4. n _ _ ther

5. s _ _ ze

6. th _ _ f

7. fr _ _ nd

8. ch _ _ f

9. c _ _ ling

10. p _ _ ce

Mostly <u>ie</u> and <u>ei</u> make an **e** sound.
But in words that end in **d** they make an **i** sound: like **d<u>ie</u>d**.

11

■ TEST 2 ■

Sound-alikes

Cross out the word that's wrong:

1 I get | four/for | pounds a week pocket money.

2 The | whole/hole | building blew up.

3 The book was written | buy/by | Roald Dahl.

4 What have they done with | their/there | shoes?

5 Do you | no/know | what time it is?

ie or ei?

Fill in the gaps with **ie** or **ei**:

6 l _ _ d   **8** dec _ _ ve   **10** sh _ _ ld

7 pat _ _ nt   **9** rec _ _ pt   **11** n _ _ ghbour

Plural endings

Write the plurals of these:

12 stick___   **17** bike___   **22** wish___

13 ash___   **18** toe___   **23** sandwich___

14 bunch___   **19** night___   **24** volcano___

15 fox___   **20** watch___   **25** loss___

16 kiss___   **21** cargo___

Score 1 each.

SCORE

25

More sound-alikes

Which is which
... or witch?

Look at these:

witch	The **witch** rides on a broomstick.
which	**Which** way do I go?
peace	**Peace** is when there is no war.
piece	A **piece** of the jigsaw is missing.
blue	The sky is **blue**, the grass is green.
blew	The wind **blew** the tree down.
where	**Where** are we going on holiday?
wear	You can't **wear** that shirt, it's dirty.
of	Grandpa gave me a bag **of** sweets.
off	Dad fell **off** the stepladder.

These two words
don't sound quite the
same, but they are
often muddled up.

Now try using them over the page. **13**

More sound-alikes

Put the correct word in the gap.

1. The _____ had a black cat. (witch/which)

2. Can I have a _____ of cake? (peace/piece)

3. _____ are my jeans?. (where/wear)

4. I fell _____ the chair. (off/of)

5. All I want is some _____ and quiet. (peace/piece)

6. There are a lot _____ apples on the tree. (off/of)

7. _____ is your bag? (witch/which)

8. The wind _____ the roof off the shed. (blue/blew)

9. I am going to _____ my new dress. (wear/where)

10. The sun is shining and the sea is _____. (blue/blew)

Now **cover** over the top of the page and see if you can spell all ten words from **memory**. (If you get stuck, ask someone to read them to you.)

1. _____   6. _____

2. _____   7. _____

3. _____   8. _____

4. _____   9. _____

5. _____   10. _____

More spell as you see

Another twenty useful words to know.
When you've learnt a word, fire the rocket!

Start again if you
get it wrong!

Learn ten today ...   ... and ten tomorrow.

want

trouble

valuable

enough

again

ceiling

different

goes

first

holiday

next

really

little

picture

join

invite

minute

quarter

often

knife

15

More plural endings

Look at these two words. They both end with **y**, but how are they different?

monkey

The plural of monkey is monk**eys**.

baby

The plural of baby is bab**ies**.

If a word ends in **y** with a **vowel** in front (like monk**e**y) you just add **s**.
If a word ends in **y** with a **consonant** in front (like ba**b**y)
you change the **y** to **i** and add **es**.

Remember that
the vowels are
a e i o u ...

... all the rest
are consonants.

Now try these.
Put the plural in the box.   Like this: **story** | **stories** |

1. **day**

6. **country**

2. **jelly**

7. **lorry**

3. **trolley**

8. **toy**

4. **chimney**

9. **fairy**

5. **robbery**

10. **butterfly**

■ TEST 3 ■

To the adult: Using a separate piece of paper, test the spellings learnt on page 15. Score 1 for each correct word: and practise any spelt incorrectly.

SCORE

/20

More spelling by rules

When a word ends with **e** and you add

| **–ing** | or | **–ed** | or | **–er** | you drop the **e**. |

For example:

| dance | dan<u>cing</u> | dan<u>ced</u> | dan<u>cer</u> |

Add the endings to these words:

	–ing	**–ed**	**–er**
lose			
take			
save			
use			
love			
drive			
hope			
time			

■ TEST 4 ■

Fill the gaps with the correct **sound-alike** word.

1 [_____] **did I put my watch?** (wear/where)

2 [_____] **cake would you like?** (which/witch)

3 I took the lid [_____] **the jar.** (of/off)

4 Please can I have a [_____] **of bread?** (piece/peace)

5 I [_____] **up the balloons for the party.** (blew/blue)

Add the **endings** to these words:

	−ing	**−ed**	**−er**
dive	**6**	**7**	**8**
mine	**9**	**10**	**11**
shave	**12**	**13**	**14**

Write the **plurals** to these words:

15 reply [_____]   **18 fly** [_____]

16 copy [_____]   **19 tray** [_____]

17 day [_____]   **20 lolly** [_____]

Score I each.

18

More spell as you see

Learn the spellings for the months of the year
and the days of the week.
Cross out ✗ on the calendar when you've learnt
each word.

*... and keep doing it
until you get it right!*

Learn these today!

January	February	March
April	May	June
July	August	September
October	November	December

... and these tomorrow!

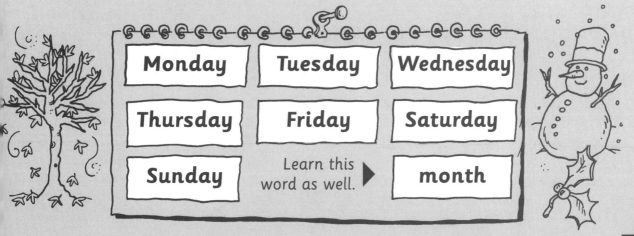

Monday	Tuesday	Wednesday
Thursday	Friday	Saturday
Sunday	Learn this word as well. ▶	month

19

More spelling by rules

When you have a word like **plan** ◀ one consonant at end
vowel ▲

and you want to add [**–ing**] or [**–ed**] or [**–er**],

you must double the last letter:
pla<u>nn</u>ing   pla<u>nn</u>ed   pla<u>nn</u>er

except when the word ends in **w**, **x**, or **y**.
blo<u>w</u>ing   ta<u>x</u>ed   pla<u>y</u>er

Now fill in the missing words in this table.

	–ing	–ed	–er
stop			
begin			
swim			
stay			
dig			
box			
rob			
mow			

Silent letters

Look out for these letters. They may be **silent**.

w	h	b	g	gh	final	e	k

You don't say **silent** letters when reading,
but you have to write them when you're spelling.

For example:

wrap	**w**here	de**b**t	sign fight wine	**k**nee
▲	▲	▲	▲ ▲ ▲	▲
before an **r** or sometimes at the end:	but sometimes:	before a **t** or after an **m**:	These three make the vowel **i** say its own name.	Before an **n**.
▼	▼	▼		
lo**w**	**w**hole	bom**b**		

Put a ring round the silent letters in these words, and **learn** the spellings.

knot	cake	sigh
made	what	night
wrist	tune	gnome

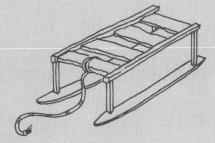

flight	design	thumb
who	doubt	sleigh
wrong	knit	know
when	whose	receipt

To the adult: Using a separate piece of paper, test the spellings learnt on page 19. Score 1 for each correct word: and practise any spelt incorrectly.

SCORE

/20

Special plurals

Three more ways to make plurals:

Words ending in **f** or **fe** drop the f (or fe) and add **ves**

thief → thieves   **wife → wives**

<u>**except**</u>   chief → chiefs   roof → roofs

... and one of the words on page 23 ▶

Some words (very few) don't change at all!

one sheep → six sheep

one deer → a lot of deer

one salmon → many salmon

Some words change their spelling (and sound different).

mouse → mice

woman → women

tooth → teeth

child → children

But the plural of **house** is **houses**!

22

Special plurals

Fill in the plurals of these words:

1 dwarf ▶

2 dormouse ▶

3 calf ▶

4 loaf ▶

5 man ▶

6 lamb ▶   this is a trick one!

7 hoof ▶

8 leaf ▶

9 hive ▶

10 wolf ▶

11 scarf ▶

12 goose ▶

13 aircraft ▶

14 shelf ▶

15 series ▶

■ TEST 6 ■

Fill in the gaps.

	–ing	–ed	–er
signal	❶	❷	❸
kidnap	❹	❺	❻
travel	❼	❽	❾
paint	❿	⓫	⓬

Write in the **plurals**.

⓭ *foot* ▶

⓮ *life* ▶

⓯ *half* ▶

⓰ *louse* ▶

⓱ *stamp* ▶

Draw a ring round the **silent** letters.

⓲ **white** ㉑ **light** ㉔ **reign**

⓳ **whole** ㉒ **crumb** ㉕ **knock**

⓴ **wreck** ㉓ **tow**

Score I each.

24

More spell as you see

REMEMBER: Look – Copy – Cover – Write – Check

Another twenty useful words to know.
Learn ten today and ten tomorrow.

Pick the apple when you've learnt the word.

Start again if
you get it
wrong!

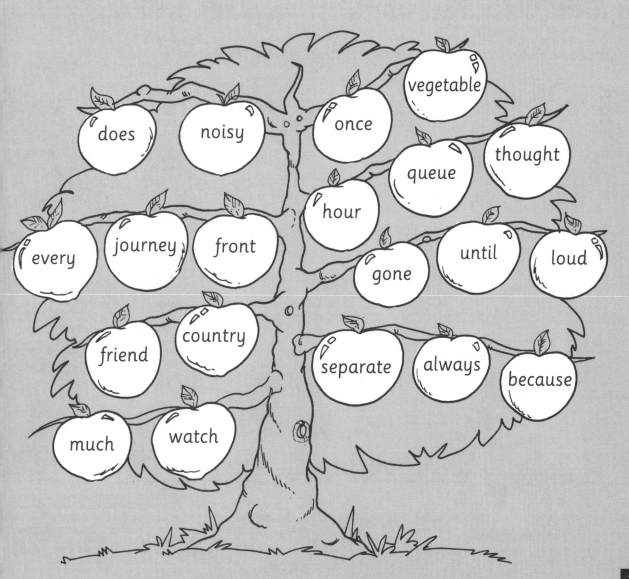

- vegetable
- does
- noisy
- once
- thought
- queue
- hour
- every
- journey
- front
- until
- loud
- gone
- friend
- country
- separate
- always
- because
- much
- watch

Word beginnings

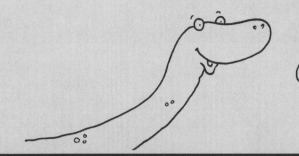

People often get these wrong. But the rule is simple!

When you add **dis–** or **mis–** or **un–** , never add or take away a letter at the join.

For example:

un + necessary = u<u>nn</u>ecessary
dis + appear = di<u>s</u>appear
mis + spell = mi<u>ss</u>pell

Now try these:

1. dis + satisfy
2. mis + understood
3. un + do
4. mis + shapen
5. dis + approve

6. un + afraid
7. mis + behave
8. un + noticed
9. mis + lead
10. dis + appoint

Talking spelling

People don't talk like a book.
So when you write down how people speak, you spell the words
in a special way.

Like this:

▼ apostrophe
I'm = I am
▲ missing letter

I'll = I shall / will
it's = it is / it has
she'll = she will
we're = we are
you're = you are
you'll = you will
they're = they are
they'll = they will
shan't = shall not

Where the letters are missed out,
you put a mark high up called
an **apostrophe**

won't = will not
aren't = are not
can't = cannot
didn't = did not
don't = do not
doesn't = does not
isn't = is not

■ TEST 7 ■

To the adult: Using a separate piece of paper, test the spellings learnt on
page 25. Score 1 for each correct word: and practise any spelt incorrectly.

More talking spelling

Use a red pen and put the talking spellings in these sentences.
Like this:

isn't   won't
It is not right so I will not do it.

I am sorry he did not come.

She will not play because she cannot run!

It does not matter that it is not finished.

They did not come to see you because you are so mean!

I am sure it is not your fault!

It is a pity we did not see the princess arrive.

I shall not eat it and you will not because <u>they</u> did not eat it!

More sound-alikes

are	You **are** my best friend.
our	Will you join **our** team?
your	Where is **your** house?
you're	**You're** a clever girl.
right	If you turn **right** at the crossroads, you will be going the **right** way.
write	Please **write** your name on this card.
hear	You **hear** with your ear.
here	I put it **here** in this place.
wood	Trees are made of **wood**.
would	I **would** like a bike.
threw	He **threw** a ball
through	He went **through** the door

> Remember – you can have the **right** spelling for the **wrong** word.

Now check these sound-alikes.

Tick ✔ the word if it is right. Put a cross ✘ if it is wrong.

1. Will you   write   you're   name   hear   ?

2. How many of   are   hens   are   missing?

3.   Your   not getting it   right   .

4.   Wood   you run   through   the dark   would   ?

5. I can   here   a dog barking   threw   the wall.

■ TEST 8 ■

Add these beginnings: | un– | dis– | mis– | to the words below:

1 _ _ like

5 _ _ happy

8 _ _ expected

2 _ _ _ take

6 _ _ used

9 _ _ _ understand

3 _ _ needed

7 _ _ _ lay

10 _ _ _ comfort

4 _ _ _ solve

Score I each.

SCORE

/ 10

Spell as you see

REMEMBER: Look – Copy – Cover – Write – Check

▼

Last of all – another twenty useful words to know.
Learn ten today and ten tomorrow.

Start again if you get it wrong!

When you've learnt the word, cross it out.

before

business

yesterday

should

sincerely

juice

straight

useful

rhyme

busy

answer

another

tomorrow

foreign

lonely

nowhere

other

excited

usually

30

■ TEST 9 ■

Give the **talking spellings** of these words without looking at page 27.
Then check them to see if you're right.

1 did not   = [   ]   **6** they are = [   ]

2 she will   = [   ]   **7** cannot   = [   ]

3 does not = [   ]   **8** is not   = [   ]

4 we are   = [   ]   **9** it is   = [   ]

5 shall not = [   ]   **10** you are = [   ]

Put a tick ✔ or a cross ✗ against these **sound-alikes**.

11 Take the first turning on the [write] and go

[through] the park.

12 [Hear] is the box you [through] away.

13 Will you [right] a letter to [your] grandma?

14 I [would] put [our] computer over [hear] .

15 I made [you're] go-kart out of some [wood] in

[are] garage.

16 – 35 To the adult: Using a separate sheet of paper, test the 20 spellings learnt on page 30. Score 1 for each correct word: and practise any spelt incorrectly.

SCORE

/ 35

Answers

Page 2
cat dog pin hat jug; tin pig cot
van sun; tap bat rat axe hen;
egg peg mop zip web

Page 3
television motorbike helicopter
kangaroo octopus butterfly
caterpillar trampoline chocolate
rollerskates calculator daffodil

Page 6
1 father knee 2 early caught 3 Many
exercise 4 address said 5 interest
around

Page 9
1 four 2 buy 3 their 4 no 5 whole 6
by 7 for 8 hole 9 there 10 know

1 four 2 by 3 know 4 there 5 whole

Page 10
1 tomato<u>es</u> 6 taps   11 address<u>es</u>
2 wish<u>es</u>   7 tables   12 torch<u>es</u>
3 echo<u>es</u>   8 princess<u>es</u> 13 shoes
4 windows   9 fox<u>es</u>   14 match<u>es</u>
5 presents   10 brush<u>es</u> 15 bus<u>es</u>

Page 11
1 dec<u>ei</u>ve   6 th<u>ie</u>f
2 t<u>ie</u>d   7 fr<u>ie</u>nd
3 f<u>ie</u>ld   8 ch<u>ie</u>f
4 n<u>ei</u>ther   9 c<u>ei</u>ling
5 s<u>ei</u>ze   10 p<u>ie</u>ce

TEST 2   Page 12
(correct words): 1 four 2 whole 3 by
4 their 5 know

6 lied   8 dec<u>ei</u>ve   10 shield
7 patient   9 rec<u>ei</u>pt   11 n<u>ei</u>ghbour

12 sticks   17 bikes   22 wish<u>es</u>
13 ash<u>es</u>   18 toes   23 sandwich<u>es</u>
14 bunch<u>es</u>   19 nights   24 volcano<u>es</u>
15 fox<u>es</u>   20 watch<u>es</u>   25 losses
16 kiss<u>es</u>   21 cargo<u>es</u>

Page 14
1 witch 2 piece 3 where 4 off
5 peace 6 of 7 which 8 blew 9 wear
10 blue

Page 16
1 day<u>s</u> 2 jell<u>ies</u> 3 trolley<u>s</u> 4 chimney<u>s</u>
5 robber<u>ies</u>

6 countr<u>ies</u> 7 lorr<u>ies</u> 8 toy<u>s</u> 9 fair<u>ies</u>
10 butterfl<u>ies</u>

TEST 3   Page 17
losing loser; taking taker;
saving saved saver; using used user;
loving loved lover; driving driver;
hoping hoped; timing timed timer

TEST 4   Page 18
1 where 2 which 3 off 4 piece 5 blew;
6 diving 7 dived 8 diver
9 mining 10 mined 11 miner
12 shaving 13 shaved 14 shaver
15 replies 16 copies 17 days 18 flies
19 trays 20 lollies

Page 20
stopping stopped stopper;
beginning beginner;
swimming swimmer; staying stayed;
digging digger; boxing boxed boxer;
robbing robbed robber;
mowing mowed mower

Page 21
(k)not cak(e) si(gh); mad(e) w(h)at
ni(gh)t; (w)rist tun(e) (g)nome; fli(gh)t
desi(g)n thum(b); (w)ho dou(b)t
slei(gh); (w)rong (k)nit (k)now;
w(h)en (w)hose recei(p)t

Page 23
1 dwarfs 2 dormice 3 calves
4 loaves 5 men 6 lambs 7 hoofs or
hooves 8 leaves 9 hives 10 wolves
11 scarves 12 geese 13 aircraft 14
shelves 15 series

TEST 6   Page 24
1 signalling 2 signalled 3 signaller
4 kidnapping 5 kidnapped
6 kidnapper
7 travelling 8 travelled 9 traveller
10 painting 11 painted 12 painter
13 feet 14 lives 15 halves 16 lice
17 stamps

18 w(h)ite   21 li(gh)t   24 rei(g)n
19 (w)hole   22 crum(b)   25 (k)nock
20 (w)reck   23 to(w)

Page 26
1 dissatisfy 2 misunderstood 3 undo
4 misshapen 5 disapprove 6 unafraid
7 misbehave 8 unnoticed 9 mislead
10 disappoint

Page 28
I'm sorry he didn't come. She won't
play because she can't run! It doesn't
matter that it's not finished. They
didn't come to see you because you're
so mean. I'm sure it's not your fault!
It's a pity we didn't see the princess
arrive. I shan't eat it and you won't
because <u>they</u> didn't eat it!

Page 29
(correct words): 1 Will you write your
name here? 2 How many of our hens
are missing? 3 You're not getting it
right. 4 Would you run through the
dark wood? 5 I can hear a dog
barking through the wall.

TEST 8
Page 30
1 <u>dis</u>- (or <u>un</u>-) like 2 <u>mis</u>take
3 <u>un</u>needed 4 <u>dis</u>solve 5 <u>un</u>happy
6 <u>dis</u>- (or <u>mis</u>- or <u>un</u>-) used 7 <u>mis</u>lay
8 <u>un</u>expected 9 <u>mis</u>understand
10 <u>dis</u>comfort

TEST 9
Page 31
1 didn't 2 she'll 3 doesn't 4 we're
5 shan't 6 they're 7 can't 8 isn't
9 it's 10 you're

(correct words): 11 Take the first
turning on the <u>right</u> and go <u>through</u> the
park.
12 <u>Here</u> is the box you <u>threw</u> away.
13 Will you <u>write</u> a letter to <u>your</u>
grandma?
14 I <u>would</u> put our computer over
<u>here</u>.
15 I made <u>your</u> go-kart out of some
<u>wood</u> in <u>our</u> garage.

Published by Hodder Children's Books, a division of Hodder Headline plc,
338 Euston Road, London NW1 3BH.
Printed and bound in Great Britain by The Devonshire Press Ltd, Barton Rd, Torquay.
A CIP record is registered by and held at the British Library

Reading

AGE 7-9

Dr Bill Gillham

Illustrated by Sascha Lipscomb

At this age children can quickly catch up with reading – it's more difficult later on. This book is designed to focus on the basic skills needed for reading: the different ways of recognising words. In English no 'rule' about letters and sounds is 100% true. But if it works 90–95% of the time it's worth using.

How to help your child

● Keep sessions short and regular: learning is better when it is spaced out.

● Make sure your child understands what they have to do.

● Encourage your child to ask for help, but give it by asking questions rather than telling the answer.

● Ask your child to show you what they have done: point out mistakes briefly and **praise what they've got right!**

● Don't treat the tests too formally. They are designed to make your child aware of their progress and give them a sense of achievement.

● Remember: fluent reading comes from practice with books that children find **easy**. Use the nine out of ten rule. Ask them to read you a page; if they get more than one word in ten wrong, it's too hard.

*Hodder
Children's
Books*

The only home learning programme supported by the NCPTA

Letters and sounds

Put a tick under each one that you know.

Practise any you're not sure of.

Remember –
a letter's **sound**
isn't the same as
its **name**.

a	b	c	d	e

f	g	h	i	j	k	l

m	n	o	p	q	r	s

t	u	v	w	x	y	z

a e i o u are all VOWELS
(and so is **y** when it comes at the end of a word).
All other letters are called CONSONANTS.

2

First letter sounds

Write down the first letter sounds for these pictures, like this:

Practise any you get wrong.

b

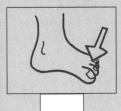    

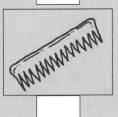 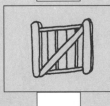 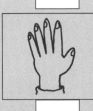  

 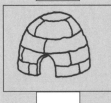 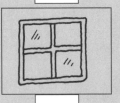 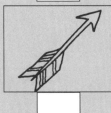 

  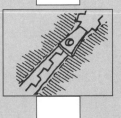  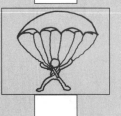

  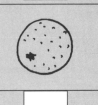  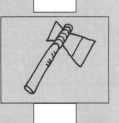

Write down the letter sound
in the **middle** of this word.

3

Special letters

Some letters make **two** sounds.

a	as in	(a)pple	or	[a] lien	
c	as in	(c)up	or	[c] ity	
e	as in	(e)gg	or	[e] lastic	
g	as in	(g)ap	or	[g] inger	
i	as in	(i)nk	or	[i] ron	
o	as in	(o)range	or	[o] pen	
u	as in	(u)nder	or	[u] niform	

And this one makes **three.**

y   as in   (y)o-yo   or   b[y]   or   sadl⟨y⟩

But only at the **end** of a word!

Match these words by their
first sounds to the ones in the boxes:

ugly   carpet   enemy   acid

circle   even   gin

on   island   acre   good

invent   unit   only   yellow

Write them here: ▼

apple		orange		ginger	
cup		under		iron	
egg		alien		open	
gap		city		uniform	
ink		elastic		yo-yo	

4

Which sound?

Read the first two words in this row:

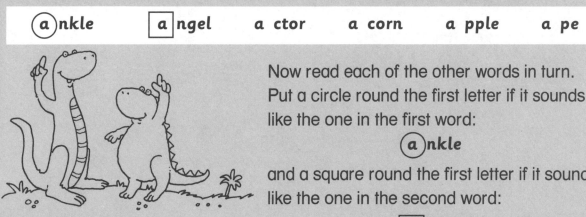

| (a)nkle | [a]ngel | a ctor | a corn | a pple | a pe |

Now read each of the other words in turn.
Put a circle round the first letter if it sounds like the one in the first word:

(a)nkle

and a square round the first letter if it sounds like the one in the second word:

[a]ngel

Now do the same with these:

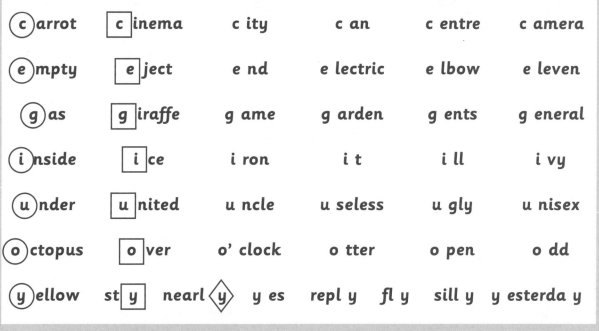

(c)arrot	[c]inema	c ity	c an	c entre	c amera
(e)mpty	[e]ject	e nd	e lectric	e lbow	e leven
(g)as	[g]iraffe	g ame	g arden	g ents	g eneral
(i)nside	[i]ce	i ron	i t	i ll	i vy
(u)nder	[u]nited	u ncle	u seless	u gly	u nisex
(o)ctopus	[o]ver	o' clock	o tter	o pen	o dd
(y)ellow	st[y] nearl◇y◇	y es	repl y	fl y	sill y	y esterda y

Put a **diamond** round the third sound y makes.

5

Special sounds

Some consonants make a different sound when there are two of them together.

Here are the most common ones:

ch	as in	**ch**imney
sh	as in	**sh**op
th	as in	**th**at (hard)
		think (soft)

These make sounds you don't expect:

ph	makes a **f** sound	as in	**ph**one
ch	makes a **c** sound	as in	**ch**emist
gh	makes a **g** sound	as in	**gh**ost
wh	makes a **w** sound	as in	**wh**en
	or a **h** sound	as in	**wh**o

There are not many of these.

Mostly you just don't sound the **h** at all.

what   where   ghost   chemist

In these words you don't sound the **w**.

whose   who   whole

Put the right two-letter sounds at the beginnings of the words below.

Choose from: | th | sh | wh | ph | ch |

Like this: | __ch__ ip |

| ____in | ____ank | ____oto | ____ick | ____ampoo |

| ____eat | ____ild | ____elf | ____eep | ____ich |

Now put a circle round the two-letter sounds in these sentences.

For example: (sh) eet

When the sailor fell off his
ship, a shark ate him up.

My little brother ate
a whole box of chocolates.

A chimney fell off our roof
when there was a gale.

I saw three pheasants while
I was out walking.

7

Word endings

You don't sound the *e*
- **-le** as in hand**le**
- **-el** as in parc**el**
- **-ed** as in kick**ed**

You don't sound the *o* ▶ **-our** as in col**our**

You don't sound the *a* ▶ **-ar** as in calend**ar**

They all say **shun**
- **-shion** as in cu**shion**
- **-sion** as in televi**sion**
- **-tion** as in sta**tion**

Soft **c**: you don't sound the *e* ▶ **-ce** as in dan**ce**

You don't sound the *o* ▶ **-ous** as in fam**ous**

You only sound the *t* ▶ **-ght** as in ni**ght**

You don't sound it at all ▶ **-gh** as in si**gh**

Says *f* ▶ **-gh** as in rou**gh**

Am I hi**gh** enou**gh**?

8

Put the right endings to complete these words.

Choose from here:

ght	tion	gh	ar	el	ous
our	sion	ed	ce	le	shion

ang___

danger___

cu___

arm___

fi___

cou___

hi___

jew___

sta___

begg___

thou___

tremend___

min___

sadd___

peop___

vineg___

tou___

fa___

televi___

turn___

preci___

lo___

brou___

Sometimes more than one ending will fit!

Word beginnings

Choose from these: | th | sh | wh | ph | ch |

1 ____ocolate   **2** ____ed   **3** ____one   **4** ____o   **5** ____ey

6 ____imble   **7** ____adow   **8** ____ite   **9** ____eek   **10** ____alk

Look at these pictures. What two letters do the words begin with?
Write them underneath.

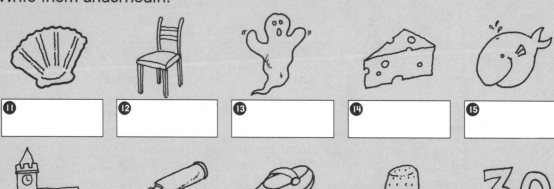

11   **12**   **13**   **14**   **15**

16   **17**   **18**   **19**   **30**

Word endings

Choose from these:

ght	tion	gh	er	ly	ous
ing	sion	ed	ce	ay	shion

21 push____   **22** lau____   **23** ti____   **24** poor____   **25** pow____   **26** na____

27 fa____   **28** str____   **29** explo____   **30** enorm____   **31** pl____   **32** prin____

SCORE

32

Vowel pairs

Sort the words in the circles into the right columns.

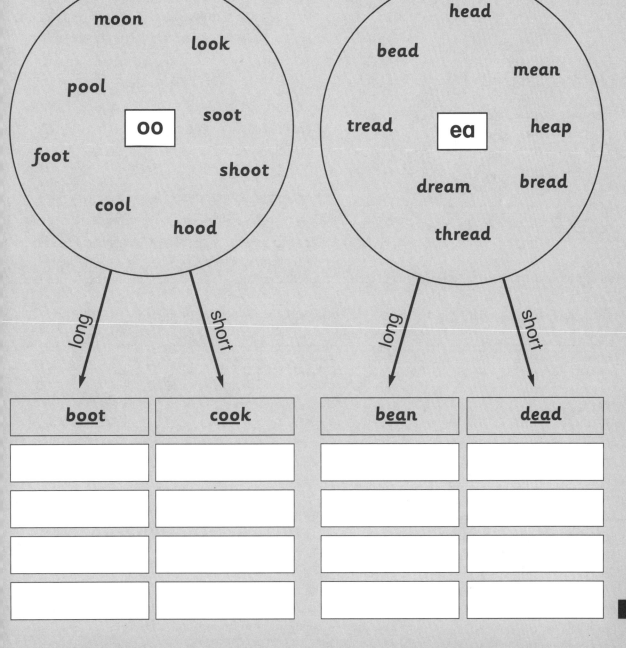

More vowel pairs

Can you see these vowel pairs in this story? Put a ring round them.

Gregg checked the nylon chain that joined him to the space station. It was okay. He could stay outside long enough to check the oil inlet. The side of the station was steep, but his load of tools was nothing in zero gravity. He pushed with his heel and floated up. The rays of the sun were bright: he couldn't see very well. No time to waste: the Martian fleet was on its way.

Look at these pictures. Write the vowel pairs for each word underneath.

ee

12

There is more than one way of saying these vowel pairs.

ie   **ou**   **ow** ◀ Not a vowel but sounds like one.

ie says the name of the first vowel, **i** ...

ie

... except when it says the name of the second vowel, **e**.

ou says **ow** ...

ou

... except when it comes before **gh** or **ld**.

and **ow** says **ow** ...

ow

... except when it says **oh**.

ou is the one to watch!

Find four more like these:

l<u>ie</u>	ch<u>ie</u>f	l<u>ou</u>d	c<u>ow</u>	l<u>ow</u>

There is more about **ou** on the next page.

ough   **ould**

This one's the worst!

When you see these in a word WATCH OUT!

There are four ways of saying **ough**.

cough   says   **c**off   Think of another word like it. ▶

though   says   th**oh**   another like it ▶

en**ough**   says   en**uff**   another like it ▶

though**t**   says   th**aw**t   another like it ▶

There are two ways of saying **ould**.

In this one you say the **u** but not the **o**. ▶ **c**ould   **b**oulde**r** ◀ In this one you say the **o** but not the **u**.

Now think of two more of each.

■ TEST 2 ■

Vowel pairs

ie	ee	oi	oo	oa
ow	ai	ay	ou	ea

Fit the vowel pairs into the gaps in these words.

1 t____gh

2 fl_____

3 c____t

4 t____k

5 p____n

6 t____n

7 t____d

8 n____d

9 w____ld

10 m____n

11 f____l

12 p_____

13 c____n

14 h____se

15 r____d

Look for the same vowel pairs in this story and put a ring round them.
Score 1 for each vowel pair you find.

The room was grey in the moonlight. The only sound Karen could hear was the beating of her heart. Why had she stayed? Was there really a ghost? She needed to know. She pulled her coat round her and tied the belt. Still no sound. Then a loud bang as the main door burst open, the noise echoing through the rooms.

SCORE

36

15

The final 'e' rule

When there's an 'e' at the end of a word, the 'e' has no sound.
But it makes the vowel before it say its name.

not / note

Shh!

hid / hide

What did you say your name was?

Here are some more examples:

hat → hate

cod → code

hop → hope

fad → fade

See how the final 'e' changes the meaning.

Now add the 'e' to these words and say the new words as you do it.

spin

cap

rob

dam

bit

pan

rat

pip

Now think of some for yourself.

If you get stuck, see the ones in the answers on page 32.

	→		→
	→		→
	→		→
	→		→

Think of the words to go with these pictures:

Say them in your head.

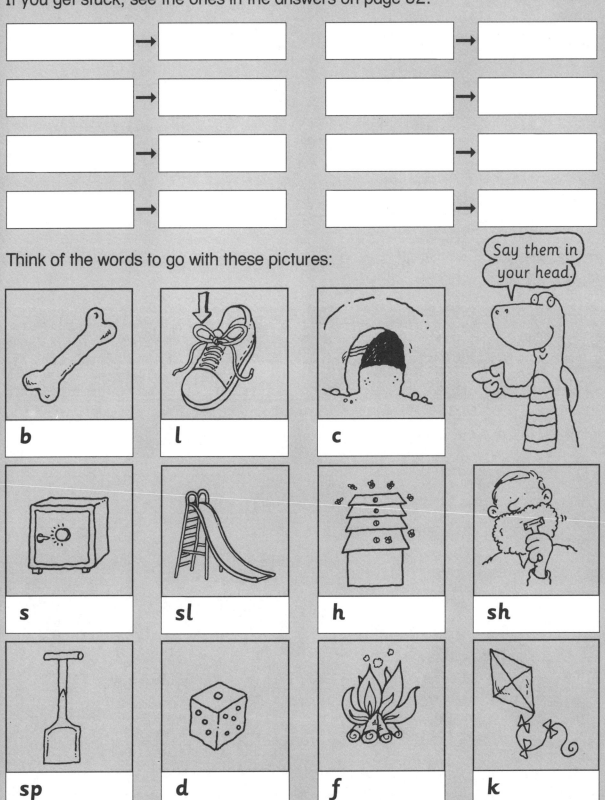

b

l

c

s

sl

h

sh

sp

d

f

k

How to read big words

The 'little words' in big words are called

syllables

Here's a big word broken up into syllables:

pre|his|tor|ic

and another

di|no|saur

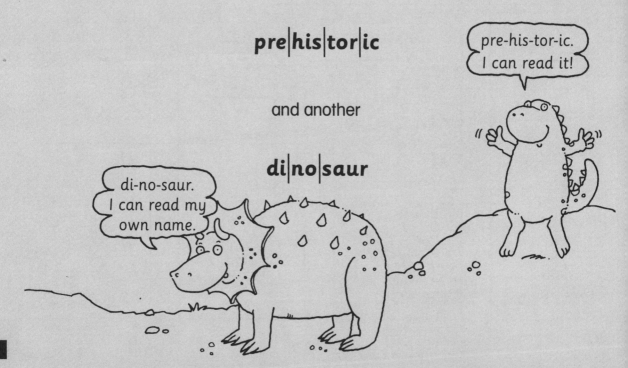

Here are the rules.

● A syllable has to sound like a little word but it doesn't have to be a proper word.

op|po|site

There isn't such a thing as an **op**!

● It has to have at least one vowel in it (a, e, i, o, u, y).

↓ ↓ ↓
in|ter|est

Every syllable has a vowel.

● Sometimes a vowel is a syllable on its own.

↓
e|lec|tric

That's a short syllable!

● When there are two consonants together the break usually comes in the middle ...   **pot|ter**

● ... except when they make a sound together.

fa|ther   **fat|head**
   ↑   ↑↑
one sound   separate sounds

● Otherwise the break usually comes before the consonant.

stu|pid   **cle|ver**

Which one are you?

19

Syllables

Now try these.

Put the syllables in the boxes.

Two syllables

empty

Like this ▶ | emp | ty |

prison

| | |

carpet

| | |

broken

| | |

protect

| | |

stupid

| | |

appear

| | |

inside

| | |

dislike

| | |

mistake

| | |

brother

| | |

biscuit

| | |

Three syllables

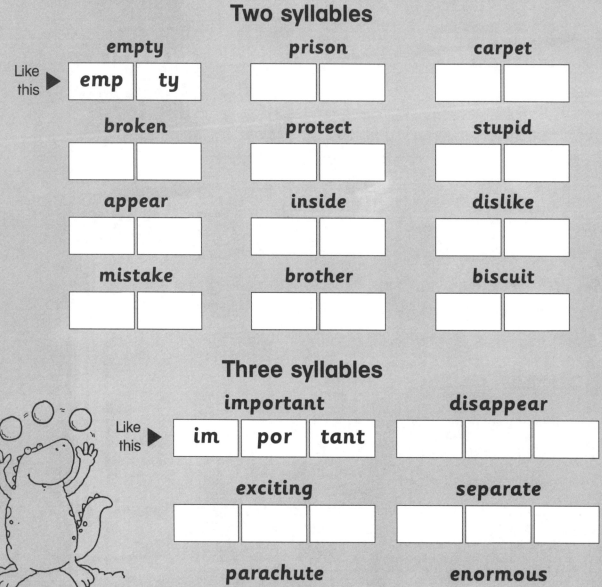

important

Like this ▶ | im | por | tant |

disappear

| | | |

exciting

| | | |

separate

| | | |

parachute

| | | |

enormous

| | | |

And now for four syllables.

Take your time!
Say the syllables slowly in your head.

That's me!

intelligent

disappointment

interesting

unimportant

unexpected

That's **not** me!

ridiculous

electronic

expedition

operation

accidental

Make your own words

So now you can break up words. Let's see if you can put them together!

Make up 10 two-syllable words from these:

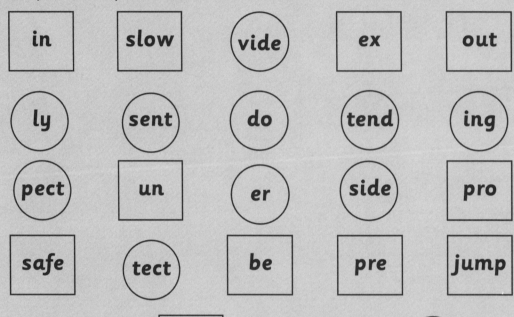

in	slow	vide	ex	out
ly	sent	do	tend	ing
pect	un	er	side	pro
safe	tect	be	pre	jump

Word beginnings are in squares. Word endings are in circles.

You can use the same syllable more than once.

1. ☐ ☐   6. ☐ ☐

2. ☐ ☐   7. ☐ ☐

3. ☐ ☐   8. ☐ ☐

4. ☐ ☐   9. ☐ ☐

5. ☐ ☐   10. ☐ ☐

■ TEST 3 ■

Break up the words by drawing lines down like this:

an|nu|al

The numbers in the squares tell you how many syllables there are.

2	3	2	3
shower	stepladder	upset	amazing

4	2	2	2
television	washing	breakfast	pillow

4	3	3	3
excavation	stereo	presently	underground

Put the syllables in the boxes.

spider

butterfly

telephone

computer

operation

snuggle

envelope

formula

particular

Score 1 for each correct syllable.

Which word?

If you don't know a word, the other words in the sentence can help you work out what it is.

Like this:

Our cat caught a little _____.

I think it could be **dog**.

It could be **mouse** or it could be **bird**.

If you know how the word starts that's a big help.

Like this:

Our cat caught a little r_____.

It could be **rat** or it could be **rabbit**.

I think it could be **rhino**.

None of these is right!

Our cat caught a little ro_____.

What do **you** think it could be? See the answer on page 32.

24 Now try these on the next page.

There are three words to choose from in each of the following sentences. Only one of them is right. Put a ring round the right word.

Like this:

● Because it was raining he put a

cap
cup
can

on his head.

No points for funny answers!

1. Sam had so much to eat that he was

stick
sitting
sick

.

2. When a wheel came off the car it

crashed
crept
carried

into a wall.

3. With a pin she

burnt
burst
bought

all the children's balloons.

4. The crocodile cleaned her

toes
tomatoes
teeth

with a toothbrush.

5. The goalkeeper kicked the

bell
belt
ball

into his own goal.

Choose the word

There are ten sentences, each with a word missing.
Choose the right word to go in the gap.

| bit | snake | broke | computer |

| toast | | rocket |

| motorbike | birthday | spider | goal |

1. Our dog _____ the postman.

2. I am ten years old on my next _____.

3. I play in _____ for our football team.

4. There was a _____ with long legs in the bath.

5. When I dropped the plate it _____ into pieces.

6. I had _____ and marmalade for breakfast.

7. I like playing games with my _____.

8. My brother rides his _____ to work.

9. The _____ escaped from the zoo.

10. I went to the moon in a _____.

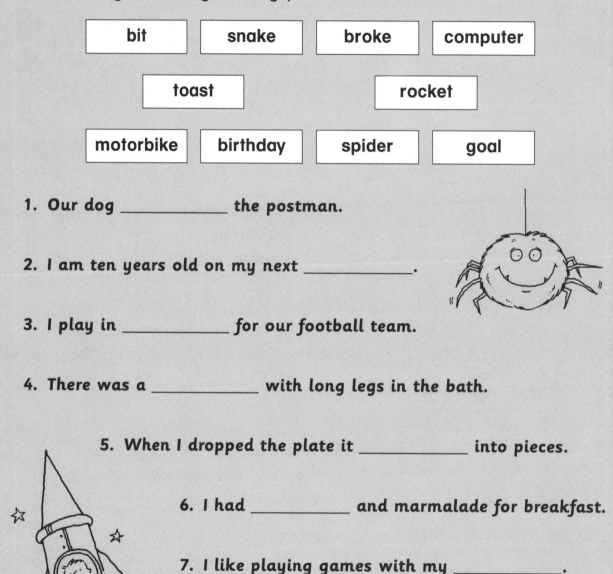

The arrow game

Each word leads to the next word.

Join up the words to make a sentence.
The first one is done for you.

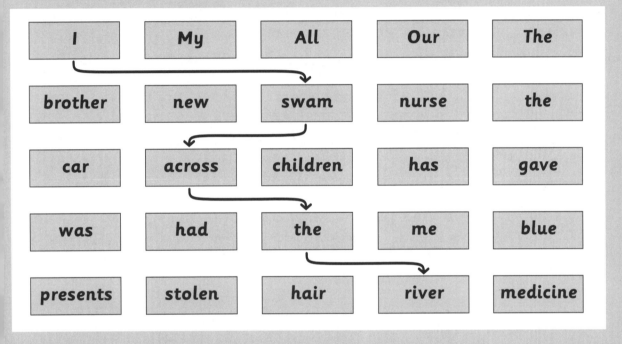

I	My	All	Our	The
brother	new	swam	nurse	the
car	across	children	has	gave
was	had	the	me	blue
presents	stolen	hair	river	medicine

Now do it across.

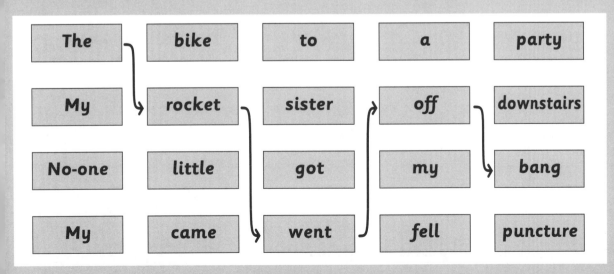

The	bike	to	a	party
My	rocket	sister	off	downstairs
No-one	little	got	my	bang
My	came	went	fell	puncture

Silly sentences

Silly sentences have the words in the wrong order like this ...

- new likes our nobody teacher.

Nobody likes our new teacher.

▲ You put them in the right order underneath.

... or a word that doesn't make sense, like this:

washing
- Dad put the dirty clothes in the ~~wishing~~ machine.

▲ You cross out the word that's wrong and put the right word in.

Now correct these 'silly sentences':

1. my lorry mum drives a big.

2. Our cat is afraid of rice.

3. caught house fire door the next.

4. I like hating fish and chips.

5. escaped a circus from the lion has.

6. I had corn flaps for breakfast.

7. my little pool into the brother fell.

8. The sky was full of dark clowns.

9. my tin thumb his opening cut a dad.

10. I dived into the slimming pool.

11. some frightened spiders of people are.

12. We picked all the angles off the tree.

13. my too big are new trainers.

14. When I was ill the donkey came to see me.

Secret letter

Here's a secret letter that has some words missing.
Fill them in to find out the message.

A sub_____ will be opposite
the li__house at midnight on
Mon___ 13th April and again
at the same ____ for three
days until you signal. Show a
light — two sh__ flashes and
one long. The code w___ is
EAGLE. Do not use a car or
carry a g__ Say you are on a
camping hol_____ but don't
talk too much to anyone. Spies
know that y__ are in the area.
Contact me only in an
em_____

008

■ TEST 4 ■

Complete or correct the following sentences:

1. I painted a [_____] of our dog.

2. Mum fried some bacon and [e_____].

3. On my birthday Dad
   | baked |
   | barked |
   | banged |
   me a cake.

4. [_____] Mum put a new tyre on the while.

5. all my face I spots over have.
   [_____]

6. I blew up the [_____] until it burst.

7. Our pet [r_____] likes carrots.

8. When the plane had taken off all the passengers had a
   | mail |
   | meal |
   | moon |
   .

9. [_____] My brother fell over and cut his hood.

10. A bee [_____] me on the arm.

11. I stuck a stamp on the [l_____].

12. I caught a
    | fork |
    | fist |
    | fish |
    with my new rod.

13. [_____] I sewed up some wood for the fire.

14. a postman parcel brought the me.
    [_____]

SCORE

31

/14

Answers

Page 3

t k n u l; c g h r f; s i w
a d; e q z y p; m v o j x

Page 4

acid, carpet, enemy, good, invent,
on, ugly, acre, circle, even,
gin, island, only, unit, yellow

Page 5

(a)ctor, (a)corn, (a)pple, (a)pe;
(c)ity, (c)an, (c)entre, (c)amera,
(e)nd, (e)lectric, (e)lbow, (e)leven;
(g)ame, (g)arden, (g)ents, (g)eneral;
(i)ron, (i)t, (i)ll, (i)vy;
(u)ncle, (u)seless, (u)gly, (u)nisex;
(o)'clock, (o)tter, (o)pen, (o)dd;
(y)es, repl(y), fl(y), sill(y), (y)esterda(y)

Page 7

(top): thin/shin/chin, thank, photo,
chick/thick, shampoo, wheat, child,
shelf, sheep, which

(bottom): (wh)en, (th)e, (sh)ip, (sh)ark;
bro(th)er, (wh)ole, (ch)ocolates;
(ch)imney, (wh)en, (th)ere;
(th)ree, (ph)easants, (wh)ile

Page 9

angle, dangerous, cushion; armour, fight,
cough; high, jewel, station; beggar,
thought, tremendous; mince, saddle,
people; vinegar, tough, fashion;
television, turned, precision; lotion,
brought (but others are possible)

TEST 1 Page 10

(top): chocolate, shed, phone, who, they;
thimble, shadow, white, cheek, chalk

(middle): shell, chair, ghost, cheese,
whale; church, whistle, shoe, thimble, thirty

(bottom): pushing/pushed, laugh, tight,
poorly, power, nation; fashion, string,
explosion, enormous, play, prince
(others possible)

Page 11

Long	Short	Long	Short
moon	foot	mean	head
pool	look	bead	tread
cool	soot	heap	bread
shoot	hood	dream	thread

Page 12

(top): chain, joined, okay, stay, oil, steep,
load, heel, floated, rays, see, fleet, way

(bottom): sheep, boat, rain, paints, tray,
coin, feet, point, coat, spray

Page 13

tie, pie, cried, tried; thief, believe, field,
shield; found, sound, house, shout; how,
town, crown, brown; tow, mow, show,
blow (and others like this)

Page 14

(top): trough, dough, rough, fought

(bottom): should, would, shoulder, mould
(and others like this)

TEST 2 Page 15

(top): tough, flea, coat, took, pain; town,
tied, need, would, mean; fool, pay, coin,
house, read (others possible)

(bottom): room, moonlight, sound, could,
hear, beating, heart, stayed, really,
needed, know, coat, round, tied, sound,
loud, main, door, noise, through, rooms

Page 16

spine, robe, bite, rate; cape, dame,
pane, pipe

Page 17

(top): fin, fine, hug, huge, sit, site, fat,
fate, kit, kite, can, cane, mad, made,
man, mane (and many others)

(bottom): bone, lace, cave; safe, slide,
hive, shave; spade, dice, fire, kite

Page 20

(two): pri son, car pet, bro ken,
pro tect, stu pid, ap pear, in side,
dis like, mis take, bro ther, bis cuit

(three): dis ap pear, ex ci ting,
sep ar ate, par a chute, e nor mous

Page 21

in tel li gent, dis ap point ment,
in ter es ting, un im por tant,
un ex pec ted, ri dic u lous, e lec tron ic,
ex pe di tion, op er a tion, ac ci den tal
(Small differences in your answers are
acceptable.)

Page 22

slowly, provide, expect, intend, undo,
jumping, safely, outside, present, beside,
protect, slower (and others like this)

TEST 3 Page 23

(top): show er, step lad der, up set,
a ma zing; tel e vi sion, wash ing,
break fast, pil low; ex ca va tion,

ste re o, pre sent ly, un der ground

(bottom): spi der, but ter fly,
tel e phone, com pu ter, o per a tion,
snug gle, en ve lope, for mu la,
par tic u lar

Page 24

robin

Page 25

1 sick, 2 crashed, 3 burst, 4 teeth, 5 ball

Page 26

1 bit, 2 birthday, 3 goal, 4 spider,
5 broke, 6 toast, 7 computer,
8 motorbike, 9 snake, 10 rocket

Page 27

(top): My brother has blue hair.
All the children had presents.
Our new car was stolen.
The nurse gave me medicine.
(bottom): My bike got a puncture.
No-one came to my party.
My little sister fell downstairs.

Page 28

1 My mum drives a big lorry.
2 Our cat is afraid of mice.
3 The house next door caught fire.
4 I like eating fish and chips.

Page 29

5 A lion has escaped from the circus.
6 I had corn flakes for breakfast.
7 My little brother fell into the pool.
8 The sky was full of dark clouds.
9 My dad cut his thumb opening a tin.
10 I dived into the swimming pool.
11 Some people are frightened of
spiders.
12 We picked all the apples off the tree.
13 My new trainers are too big.
14 When I was ill the doctor came to see
me.

Page 30

submarine, lighthouse, Monday, time,
three, short, word, gun, holiday, you,
emergency

TEST 4 Page 31

1 picture, 2 eggs, 3 baked, 4 wheel,
5 I have spots all over my face,
6 balloon, 7 rabbit, 8 meal, 9 head,
10 stung, 11 letter, 12 fish, 13 sawed,
14 The postman brought me a parcel.

Text copyright © 1996 Bill Gillham
Illustrations copyright © 1996 Sascha Lipscomb

The rights of Bill Gillham to be identified
as the author of this work has been asserted by him in
accordance with the Copyright, Design and Patent Act 1988.

First published in Great Britain 1996. Printed and bound in Great Britain.

Published by Hodder Children's Books, a division of Hodder
Headline plc, 338 Euston Road, London NW1 3BH.

A CIP record is registered by and held at the British Library.